C#

Interview Questions

You'll Most Likely Be Asked

Job Interview Questions Series

VP Vibrant Publishers

www.vibrantpublishers.com

C# Interview Questions
You'll Most Likely Be Asked

ISBN-10: 1456567667
ISBN-13: 978-14-56567-66-8

Library of Congress Control Number: 2011901173

This publication is designed to provide accurate and authoritative information in regard to the subject matter covered. The author has made every effort in the preparation of this book to ensure the accuracy of the information. However, information in this book is sold without warranty either expressed or implied. The Author or the Publisher will not be liable for any damages caused or alleged to be caused either directly or indirectly by this book.

The publisher wishes to thank Saumil Modi (India) for his invaluable inputs to this edition.

Vibrant Publishers books are available at special quantity discount for sales promotions, or for use in corporate training programs. For more information please write to **bulkorders@vibrantpublishers.com**

Please email feedback / corrections (technical, grammatical or spelling) to **spellerrors@vibrantpublishers.com**

To access the complete catalogue of Vibrant Publishers, visit **www.vibrantpublishers.com**

Contents

This page is intentionally left blank

C# Questions

Review these typical interview questions and think about how you would

answer them. Read the answers listed; you will find best possible answers

along with strategies and suggestions.

This page is intentionally left blank

OOPS - Theory

1: Does C# support *Static* Constructor?

Answer:

Yes, C# supports both *static* and instance constructor. A *Static* Constructor contains actions required to initialize a *class* when it is first loaded. An Instance Constructor contains actions required to initialize an instance of a *class*.

2: How can you implement multiple inheritances in C#?

Answer:

C# does not support multiple inheritances, one has to use interface for it.

3: C# provides default constructor, I will write my own constructor with string argument. I don't want to allow anyone from outside to call default constructor. Can I achieve it?

Answer:

Yes, you can achieve it by making it private. In such a case, no one can access this constructor.

4: Is it possible to override private virtual methods?

Answer:

No. You cannot access private method inside inherited *class*. It should be at least protected to allow its access in inherited *class*.

5: How can you make sure that your *class* can not be inherited by any other *class*?

Answer:

You can use sealed keyword. So if anyone tries to derive from your *class*, it throws an error , *cannot inherit from <given class name>`* .

6: Can you declare a private member in an Interface *Class*?

Answer:

No. In interface you are not allowed to specify any accessibility. They all are public by default.

7: Are *static* indexers allowed in C#?

Answer:

No, *Static* indexers are not allowed.

8: Can I provide different access modifiers on get/set methods of a property?

Answer:

No. We don't specify any access modifiers on *get* and *set* individually rather we specify on the wrapping property name. In other words following is valid:

```
private int m_myInt = -1;
public int MyProperty
{
  get {return m_myInt;}
  set {m_myInt = value;}
}
```

However following is not valid

```
private int m_myInt = -1;
public int MyProperty
{
  public get{return m_myInt;}
  private set{m_myInt = value;}
}
```

9: Which of the following statements is true?

A. A *class* is the implementation of an object.

B. An object is the implementation of a *class*.

C. A *class* is the instantiation of an object.

D. An object is the instantiation of a *class*.

Answer:

Correct Answer is D. When you create an object, it is called *instantiation*, and the *class* file is the blueprint for that object.

10: Is it possible to create an instance of an Abstract *Class*?
Answer:

No. You cannot create an instance of an abstract *class*. It will give compile time error.

11: Can I have a Concrete method in Abstract *Class*?
Answer:

Yes. You can have Concrete methods in Abstract *class* but you must have at least one abstract method.

12: Can I declare *Static* Variable inside Method Block?

Answer:

No. You can define *Static* variable only at *Class* level.

13: Which of the following statements are true? (Choose all that apply.)

A. Inheritance defines a contract between types.

B. Interfaces define a contract between types.

C. Inheritance derives a type from a base type.

D. Interfaces derive a type from a base type.

Answer:

Correct answers are B and C:

B. Interfaces define a contract between types, ensuring that a *class* implements specific members.

C. Inheritance derives a type from a base type, automatically implementing all members of the base *class*, while allowing the derived *class* to extend or override the existing functionality.

14: What do you mean by Interface Mapping?

Answer:

A *class* or *struct* must provide implementations of all members of the interfaces that are listed in the base *class* list of the *class* or *struct*. The process of locating implementations of interface members in an implementing *class* or *struct* is known as *Interface Mapping*.

15: What is the difference between *structs* and *classes*?

Answer:

Following are the main differences between Classes and *Structs* in C#:

a) **Value type vs Reference type:** *Structs* are value type and Classes are reference type.

  1) Whenever a *struct* object is assigned to another *struct* object a copy is created. In case of classes the same operation results in two references referring to same object.

  2) Boxing of a *struct* object creates a copy of the object in a different type, whereas, boxing a *class* object creates a reference (of different type) to the same object.

  3) Since *structs* are value types, it is not possible to assign null to a *struct* object.

  4) When a *struct* object is passed to a function as a parameter it is passed by value, unless specifically marked as 'ref' or 'out' parameter.

b) **Inheritance:** Inheritance is not allowed for *structs*.

  1) All *struct* types implicitly inherit from System.ValueType and they are implicitly sealed.

  2) The keywords related to inheritance concepts are not allowed for *structs*. For example, abstract, protected, virtual, override etc.

c) **Initialization**: *Structs* cannot have a default constructor.

1) All *struct* member variables of value type are initialized to their default values and reference member variables are initialized to null.

2) Field initializers (initialization in the member variable declaration line like int a = 6;) is not allowed for *structs*.

d) Destructor: *Structs* cannot declare a destructor.

e) Meaning of 'this':

1) For a *struct* instance constructor (parameterized) 'this' is treated as an out parameter. For other member functions it is treated as a *'ref'* parameter. So it is possible to assign to 'this' and change the current object.

2) In case of a *class* 'this' is considered as a value, so it is not possible to assign to 'this' from inside a *class*. Since 'this' is a *'ref'* or 'out' parameter, it must be definitely assigned at every point where it is used.

16: Explain scope of Private Access Modifier.

Answer:

A *class* member declared with *Private Access Modifier* will remain private to its declaring *class*. It is not accessible to any code outside its *class*, including derived classes.

17: Explain scope of Protected Access Modifier.

Answer:

A *class* member declared with *Protected Access Modifier* is accessible from within the *class* in which it is declared, and from within any *class* derived from the *class* that declared this member.

18: Explain scope of Internal Access Modifier.

Answer:

A *class* member declared with *Internal Access Modifier* is accessible only within classes in the same assembly.

19: Can we inherit *struct*?

Answer:

No. *Struct* doesn't support inheritance.

20: Is it possible to declare member as Protected in *Struct*?

Answer:

No. *Struct* doesn't support inheritance. So we cannot declare member as protected.

21: Can we declare *const* or *static* members in Interface?

Answer:

No. Interface doesn't allow constants/ fields/ operators/instance constructors, destructors, or type declaration. Interfaces consist of methods, properties, events, indexers, or any combination of these four member types.

22: Can we create an object of an Interface?

Answer:

No. Interface only allows method declaration. It doesn't provide concrete implementation. You have to implement it and you can create object of implemented type.

23: What is the difference between *Readonly* and *Const* field?

Answer:

a) A *Const* field can be initialized during declaration of a field; while *Readonly* field can be initialized either in a constructor or in field declaration.

b) The value of *const* field will be resolved during compilation; while the value of read only field will be resolved at run time.

24: What is nested type?

Answer:

A type defined within a *class* or *struct* is called *nested type.*

25: What is default accessibility of nested type?

Answer:

Default accessibility of nested type is *Private*, but can be made public, protected internal, protected, internal, or private.

26: What are Destructors?

Answer:

Destructors are used to destruct instances of classes.

27: Can we define destructor in *Struct*?

Answer:

Destructors cannot be defined in *Structs*. They are only used with classes.

28: Can we have multiple destructors in a *class*?

Answer:

No, you can only have one destructor per *class*.

29: Can we pass parameters in a destructor?

Answer:

A destructor does not take modifiers or have parameters.

30: Can we call a destructor by coding?

Answer:

A programmer has no control over when a destructor can be called because this is determined by the *garbage collector*. The garbage collector checks for objects that are no longer being used by the application. If it considers an object eligible for destruction, it calls the destructor (if any) and reclaims the memory used to store the object. *Destructors are also called when the program exits.*

31: Is overloading possible when methods have different

return types but have same signature?

Answer:

No. Overloading is not based on different return types.

32: What is Method Overloading?

Answer:

Method Overloading means you have defined same method name but different signature. Signature includes number of argument and argument type(s).

This page is intentionally left blank

OOPS - Syntax

33: Please select correct syntax for implementing Interface in C#.

(A)

Interface ITicket

{

  Int GetNoOfPendingTickets()

  {

   Int Pending = //Method for Getting data

   Return Pending;

  }

}

(B)

Interface ITicket

{

  Int GetNoOfPendingTickets();

}

(C)

Interface ITicket

{

  private int total_tickets = 0;

  Int GetNoOfPendingTickets();

}

(D)

Interface ITicket(int TotalTickets)

{

  Int GetNoOfPendingTickets(int TotalTickets);

}

Answer:

Correct Answer is B.

34: Given the following code, what will the compiler do?

```
class Test
{
  sealed abstract void MyMethod()
  {
    System.Console.WriteLine ("This is MyMethod");
  }
}
```

A. The code will compile properly.

B. The *class* visibility is incorrect.

C. System.Console.WriteLine is specified incorrectly.

D. MyMethod() is not properly declared.

Answer:

Correct Answer is D. You cannot mention sealed and abstract in the same declaration.

This page is intentionally left blank

Language - Theory

35: What is the use of *volatile* keyword?

Answer:

Volatile keyword indicates that a field can be modified in the program by something such as the operating system, the hardware, or a concurrently executing thread.

The volatile modifier is usually used for a field that is accessed by multiple threads without using the lock statement to serialize access. Using the volatile modifier ensures that one thread retrieves the most up-to-date value written by another thread.

36: What is the use of *extern modifier*?

Answer:

extern modifier is a method declaration to indicate that the method is implemented externally. Common use of the extern modifier is with the *DllImport* attribute.

37: What is the difference between extern and abstract modifier?

Answer:

extern modifier means that the method is implemented outside the C# code, while using the *abstract modifier* means that the method implementation is not provided in the *class*.

38: What is Indexer?

Answer:

An *Indexer* is a member that enables object to be indexed in the same way as an array.

39: Is the *'#include'* statement in C++ same as *'using'* statement in C#?

Answer:

No. *using* statement does not insert any code into executable, while *#include* reads the content of include file into the source file.

40: What is the output format of the file produced by the C# compiler?

A. Byte code

B. Intermediate Language (IL)

C. Hex dump

D. Intel Assembler

Answer:

B. Intermediate Language (IL)

41: Is there any difference between C++ reference and C# reference?

Answer:

Yes there is a difference. The basic idea is the same, but one significant difference is that C# references can be null. So you cannot rely on a C# reference pointing to a valid object. In that respect a C# reference is more like a C++ pointer than a C++

reference. If you try to use a null reference, a

NullReferenceException is thrown.

For example, look at the following method:

```
void displayPersonAge(person p)
{
  Console.Writeline(,Person Age is {0}'/ p.age );
}
```

The problem with this method is it will throw

NullReferenceException if called like this:

```
person p1 = null;
displayPersonAge(p1);
```

42: How can I get the name of a type at run time?

Answer:

You have to use *GetType()* method of object *class* (all types are inherited from that type).

43: How can I do case insensitive string comparison?

Answer:

For this case, you have to use *String.Compare()* method. The third argument is a Boolean represent whether cases should be ignored or not. E.g.:

```
,test` == ,Test`        \ \ False
String.Compare(,test'/ ,Test'/ True)        \ \ True
```

44: What is the difference between == and *object.Equals*?

Answer:

In case of value types, == and *object.Equals* compares two objects by value.

Int x = 1;
Int y = 1;
Console.Writeline (x == y);   \\ Output: True
Console.Writeline (x.Equals(y));   \\ Output: True

But in case of reference type, the scenario is different. In such case, == operator will return True if both references point to same object. Equal is expected to perform a value comparison, so it will return *TRUE* if the reference points to objects that are equivalent. E.g.:

StringBuilder s1 = new StringBuilder(,test');
StringBuilder s2 = new StringBuilder(,test');
Console.Writeline (s1== s2);   \\ Output: False
Console.Writeline (s1.Equals(s2));   \\ Output: True

45: What is the implicit name of the parameter that gets passed to the *class'* set method?

Answer:

The Parameter name is *value* and its type depends on the variable we are changing.

46: How many styles of commenting are supported by C#?

Answer:

C# supports three types of commenting.

    a) // used for *Single line comment*

b) /* */ used for *Multi line comment*

c) /// used for *XML documentation comments*

47: Explain the terms: Shallow copy, Deep Copy.

Answer:

a) The *Shallow Copy* copies only members of object whether they are value type or reference type. It does not copy the references which reference refers to. The reference in the new object refers to same object as old object.

b) The *Deep Copy* copies the members of an object and everything directly and indirectly referenced by the member of an object.

48: Explain the term: Immutable.

Answer:

Immutable means the data value cannot be changed. When we change data value then original data value is discarded and new data value is created in memory.

49: How can I declare Constant variable in C#?

Answer:

The keyword *const* is used to declare constant variable.

50: Can I change *const* variable in my code?

Answer:

No. When a variable is declared as a constant, it must be initialized and cannot be modified later in the application.

const int PIE = 3.142;

// PIE is now a constant with the value of 3.142

const int PIE;

// Error, a value must be provided

51: I want to initialize a constant variable, whose value is calculated on other two variables, out of which one is constant and other is a normal variable. What will happen?

Answer:

It will give an error. You can only initialize constant variable with direct value or in expression with other constant. *Const* variables can be initialized from *const* expressions.

const int x = 5;

*const int y = 8 * x; // Okay, x is known*

int A = 3; // a normal int variable

*const int z = A * x; // Error! A is not a const*

52: Given the following program, what is the outcome when you try to compile and run it?

```
using System;
class Test
{
  public static int Main()
  {
    Console.WriteLine("Hello World!");
  }
}
```

A. It will compile and print ,Hello World!` when   run.

B. It will compile and result in a runtime error indicating that the Console is an unknown object.

C. It will fail to compile with an ,error CS01610 'Test.Main( )'0 not all code paths return a value`.

D. It will fail to compile with an "error CS0161:'Test.Main( ): method cannot return an int".

Answer:

Correct Answer is C. Based on the declaration, the Main() method needs to return an integer.

53: What is the correct declaration of *static* method?

A. public *static* MethodA()

B. public void MethodA()

C. private *static* MethodA()

D. public *static* void MethodA()

Answer:

Correct Answer is D. The *static* modifier must be present as well as the return type.

54: With which of the following statement(s) you can replace *multiple if* statement in C#?

A. The *case* statement.

B. The *switch* statement.

C. The *nestedif* statement.

D. The *#endif* statement.

Answer:

Correct Answer is A. The *case* statement is the replacement for multiple nested if statements.

55: Which of the following is not a C# keyword?

A. if

B. delegate

C. private

D. MustInherit

Answer:

Correct Answer is D. The key word *MustInherit* is a Visual Basic Keyword.

56: Given the following code segment, what is the content of the string *s* in line 4?

1. string s = "Steve";

2. string j;

3. j = s;

4. r += " Joe!";

A. ‚Steve Joe!'

B. ‚Steve'

C. Nothing, it is garbage collected.

D. The code will not compile.

Answer:

Correct Answer is B. The content of *string s* will be *Steve* as *r* is not performing any operation which affects *string s.*

57: Explain the term: Implicit Conversions.

Answer:

When a variable of a smaller data type is assigned to a larger type, it is called *Implicit Conversion*. The data types must be compatible for the implicit conversion to take place.

58: Can I declare a variable called ,12Question` of type str ing in C#?

Answer:

No. In C#, an identifier must start with *a letter or an underscore*. It cannot start with a digit.

59: Can I Declare 2 variables called ,variabel1` and ,Variable1` in single method?

Answer:

Yes. C# is *Case-Sensitive*. So you can declare two variables with same name but in different case.

60: Is it necessary to write default block in Switch Statement?

Answer:

No, the default block is optional in *Switch Statement.*

61: What will be the return type of String.Compare() method?

Answer:

The Compare method Compares two specified *String* objects, ignoring or honoring their case, and returns an *integer* that indicates their relative position in the sort order.

62: Does C# support optional parameters?

Answer:

No. C# does not support optional parameters. You can get functionality of optional parameters by creating additional overloads.

63: Is it required to overload != operator when we overload == operator?

Answer:

Yes. You have to overload != operator when you overload == operator.

64: What is the use of checked & unchecked statements in C#?

Answer:

a) *Checked Statements* watch expressions for evidence of overflow. When overflow occurs, the system raises an exception.

b) *Unchecked statements* allow the overflow to proceed, undetected.

Usage:

```
using System;
public class ExceptionTester
{
 public static int Main(string[] args)
  {
```

```
int prior = 250000000;
int after = 150000000;
int total;
try
{
  checked
  {
    total = prior * after;
  }
}
catch (OverflowException oe)
{
  Console.WriteLine(, \nOverflow Message: {0}`/ oe.Message);
}
catch (Exception e)
{
  Console.WriteLine(, \nMessage: {0}`/ e.Message);
}
finally
{
  Console.WriteLine(,Finally from Main()`);
}
return 0;
}
}
```

65: In C#, can we have two classes with same name in one application?

Answer:

Yes, in C# you can declare *class* with the same name, but they must be in different namespace. In Single namespace, every *class* name must be unique.

66: What Is Type forwarding?

Answer:

Type Forwarding is an attribute (implemented in *TypeForwardedTo*) that allows you to move a type from one assembly (assembly A) into another assembly (assembly B), and to do so in such a way that it is not necessary to recompile clients that consume assembly A. After a component (assembly) ships and is being used by client applications, you can use type forwarding to move a type from the component (assembly) into another assembly and ship the updated component (and any additional assemblies required), and the client applications will still work without being recompiled. Type forwarding works only for components referenced by existing applications. When you rebuild an application, there must be appropriate assembly references for any types used in the application.

67: What is the use of sizeof operator?

Answer:

It is used to obtain the *size in bytes* for a value type.

68: Can we get size in bytes for our custom *class* with sizeof operator?

Answer:

No, sizeof operator can be only used with value types. It cannot be used with reference types.

69: Why sizeof keyword is considered as operator not a function?

Answer:

Functions are resolved at run time, while the value of size of operator is resolved at compile time. So it is more operator than a function. Also following is a correct declaration of sizeof operator.

int IntSize = sizeof int;

70: Explain *params* keyword.

Answer:

The *params* keyword lets you specify a method parameter that takes an argument where the number of arguments is variable. No additional parameters are permitted after the *params* keyword in a method declaration, and only one *params* keyword is permitted in a method declaration.

71: I want to declare a method which takes N number of arguments. How can I implement it (N will be positive integer)?

Answer:

You have to use *params* keyword for it.

72: Give any example where *params* keyword is used in method declaration.

Answer:

In C#, *Main()* Method takes variable number of arguments. Also *String.Format()* Method takes variable number of arguments.

73: What is the use of *ref* keyword?

Answer:

The *ref* keyword passes argument by reference. The effect is, any changes to the parameter in the method will be reflected in that variable when control passes back to the calling method.

74: Can we pass Value Types using *ref* keyword?

Answer:

Yes. You can pass Value Types using *ref* keyword. There is no connection between value/reference types with concept of passing by reference.

75: Is it necessary to initialize variable which will be passed by *ref* keyword?

Answer:

Yes. You have to initialize a variable which will be passed by *ref*, otherwise your program will not compile.

76: What is the use of *out* keyword?

Answer:

The *out* keyword causes arguments to be passed by reference just like *ref* keyword.

77: If both *out* and *ref* keywords pass argument by reference, what is the difference?

Answer:

Both *out* and *ref* keywords pass argument by reference bur *ref* requires the variable to be initialized before it is passed while *out* doesn't.

78: Will the following code compile?

```
class TestCalculator
{
    public void Sum(int n1, int n2, out int i) { }
    public void Sum(int n1, int n2, ref int i) { }
}
```

Answer:

No. The Code will not compile. *ref* and *out* modifiers are not considered as a part of the method signature at compile time. Therefore, methods cannot be overloaded if the only difference is that one method takes a *ref* argument and the other takes an *out* argument.

79: Can we pass properties as a method argument using *ref* or *out* modifiers?

Answer:

No. You can only pass variables using *ref* or *out* keyword.

80: What is Strong Reference?

Answer:

The garbage collector cannot collect an object in use by an application while the application's code can reach that object. In such a case, the application is said to have a *Strong Reference* to the object.

81: What is the use of *??* operator?

Answer:

The *??* operator returns the *left-hand operand* if it is not null, or else it returns the *right-hand operand*.

82: What is *Casting* or *Type Casting* or *Explicit Conversion*?

Answer:

If a conversion cannot be made without the risk of losing information, the compiler requires that you perform an *Explicit Conversion*, which is called a *Cast*. A *Cast* is a way of explicitly informing the compiler that you intend to make the conversion and that you are aware that data loss might occur. To perform a *Cast*, specify the type that you are casting to in parentheses in front of the value or variable to be converted.

83: What is the use of Explicit Keyword?

Answer:

The *Explicit Keyword* declares a user-defined type conversion operator that must be invoked with a *cast*.

For example, this operator converts from a *class* called *Foot* to a *class* called *Inch*:

```
public static explicit operator Inch(Foot f)
{
    return new Inch(f.value * 12);
}
```

This conversion operator can be invoked like this:

```
Foot f = new Foot(100.0f);
Console.Write("{0} foot", f.value);
Inch i = (Inch)f;
```

84: What is the use of ,*i s*` keyword?

Answer:

The ,*is*` keyword checks if an object is compatible with a given type. For example, the following code can determine if an object is an instance of the Ticket type, or a type that derives from Ticket

```
if (obj is Ticket)
{
  // Do Something
}
```

85: What is the use of ,*as*` keyword?

Answer:

The , *as*` operator is used to perform certain types of conversions between compatible reference types. The , *as*` operator is like a *Cast Operation*. However, if the conversion is not possible, , *as`* returns null instead of raising an *exception*. Consider following example.

```
class Parent
{
  public override string  ToString()
  {
   return "Parent";
  }
}


class Child : Parent
{ }


class Program
{
  static void Main()
  {
   Child c = new Child();
   Parent P = c as Parent;
   if (P != null)
   {
    Console.WriteLine(P.ToString());
   }
   }
}
```

86: What is the use of *?:* Operator?

Answer:

The conditional operator *?:* returns one of two values

depending on the value of a Boolean expression. Following is the syntax:

condition ? first_expression : second_expression;

If the condition is true, *first_expression* is evaluated and becomes the result. If condition is false, *second_expression* is evaluated and becomes the result. Only one of the two expressions is always evaluated.

87: What is the use of *new* modifier in method?

Answer:

The *new* keyword explicitly hides a member inherited from a base *class*. When you hide an inherited member, the derived version of the member replaces the base-class version.

88: What is the use of *yield* operator?

Answer:

The *yield* keyword signals to the compiler that the method in which it appears is an *iterator* block. The compiler generates a *class* to implement the behavior that is expressed in the *iterator* block. In the *iterator* block, the yield keyword is used together with the *return* keyword to provide a value to the enumerator object.

89: Explain the difference between *Parse, TryParse And Convert.*

Answer:

a) *Parse* will try to parse value. If it fails then it will throw an exception.

b) *TryParse* will return Boolean value based on value is parsed or not.

c) *Convert* will behave same as parse, the only difference is, incase of null value it returns default value.

90: Which namespace must be used in order to use the DOM for XML support?

A. System.Data.Xml

B. System.Xml

C. System.Xml.DOM

D. System.DOM

Answer:

The correct answer is B.

91: Which namespace will be used to perform mathematical calculations?

Answer:

System.Math

This page is intentionally left blank

Language - Syntax

92: Do these two statements generate same output?

1) string s1= ,hello \t world`

2) string s2= @,hello \t world`

Answer:

No.

  a) The first one treats '\t' as escape character and will put horizontal Tab space between hello and world.

  b) The second one treats '\t' as a normal string character.

93: What will be the output of following code segment?

class Interview

{

  static void Main()

  {

    object obj1 = ,test`;

    object obj2 = ,test`;

    system.console.writeline(obj1== obj2);

  }

}

(A) True

(B) False

Answer:

True. When two or more string literals (that are equivalent according to string equality operator) appear in the same program their string literals refer to the same string instance. Here two literals refer to the same string instance.

Data Types

94: What is *ValueType*?

Answer:

ValueType derived from *System.ValueType*, which derives from *System.Object*. *ValueType* variables directly contain their values which mean that the memory is allocated inline (stack) in whatever context the variable is declared. There is no separate heap allocation or garbage collection overhead for *value-type* variables.

95: Can we inherit *ValueType* to create new derived type?

Answer:

Value types are sealed which means that you cannot derive a type from it.

96: What is *ReferenceType*?

Answer:

A type that is defined as a *class*, delegate, array, or interface is a *Reference Type*. At run time, when you declare a variable of a reference type, the variable contains the value null until you explicitly create an instance of the object by using the new operator, or assign it an object that has been created elsewhere by using new.

When the object is created, the memory is allocated on the managed heap, and the variable holds only a reference to the location of the object.

97: What is the default value of *int* type?

Answer:

The default value of *int* type is 0 (Zero).

98: What is the default value of *bool* type?

Answer:

The default value of *bool* type is false.

99: What is the process of converting primitive type to *class* called?

A. Primitive Conversion

B. Boxing

C. Conversion

D. Encoding

E. UnBoxing

Answer:

Correct Answer is B. (*Boxing*)

Converting Value type to reference type is called *Boxing,* while converting reference type to value type is called *Unboxing.*

100: Which Data type is suitable for finance and monetary calculations?

Answer:

Decimal.

    a)   The Decimal type is a 128 bit data-type that can

represent a value ranging from 1.0×10^{-28} to approximately 7.9×10^{28} with 28-29 significant digits.

b) The float type (the 32-bit single-precision) can represent values ranging from approximately 1.5×10^{-45} to 3.4×10^{38} with a precision of 7 digits.

c) The double type (64-bit double-precision) can represent values ranging from approximately 5.0×10^{-324} to 1.7×10^{308} with a precision of 15-16 digits.

101: What is the default value of DateTime Variable?

Answer:

The default value of *DateTime is Jan 1, 0001 at 12:00 midnight.*

Here's how to create the default DateTime0

```
DateTime date = new DateTime();
Console.WriteLine(,date: {0}'/ date);
```

And the output is as follows:

date: 1/1/0001 12:00:00 AM

102: How can you get current Date and Time?

Answer:

To get current Date and Time, you have to use the method *DateTime.Now.*

103: What is the base *class* of all Enum types?

Answer:

The type *System.Enum* is the abstract base *class* of all enum types.

104: How is the Value Type stored in memory?

Answer:

Value Type is stored in *stack*.

105: How is the Reference Type stored in memory?

Answer:

Reference type is stored in *heap*.

106: Which of the following is not a Value Type? (Choose all that apply)

A. Decimal

B. String

C. System.Drawing.Point

D. Integer

E. DateTime

Answer:

The correct answer is B. String is a *Reference Type*.

107: Which of the following is not a Reference Type? (Choose all that apply)

A. Exception

B. String

C. Integer

D. Class

E. Delegate

Answer:

The correct answer is C. Integer is a *Value Type*.

Nullable Types

108: What are Nullable Types?

Answer:

Nullable Types are instances of the *System.Nullable struct.*

a) A nullable type can represent the normal range of values for its underlying value type, plus an additional null value.

b) Nullable types represent value-type variables that can be assigned the value of null.

109: Can we create a Nullable Type of Reference Type?

Answer:

You cannot create a *Nullable Type* of *Reference Type* because *Reference Types* already support the null value.

110: What are the possible values of Nullable Boolean Type?

Answer:

A *Nullable<bool>* can be assigned the values *true* or *false*, or *null*.

111: How can you check whether Nullable variable has a value or is null?

Answer:

You can use *HasValue* function of Nullable type to check this. The *HasValue* property returns *true* if the variable contains a value, or *false* if it is null.

112: What are the two possible ways of declaring Nullable

Type in C#?

Answer:

> *a)* T?

> *b)* Nullable<T>

Here T is a value type.

E.g

> *a)* int? age

> *b)* Nullable<Int> age;

113: Which of the following is the correct declaration for a nullable integer?

A. Nullable(int) i = null;

B. Nullable<int> i = null;

C. int i = null;

D. int<Nullable> i = null;

Answer:

A. *Incorrect:* The Visual Basic sample uses angle brackets rather than parentheses. The C# sample uses parentheses rather than angle brackets.

B. *Correct:* This is the proper way to declare and assign a nullable integer. In C#, you could also use the following: *int? i = null;*

C. *Incorrect:* You must use the Nullable generic to declare an integer as nullable. By default, integers are not nullable.

D. *Incorrect:* This is not the correct syntax for using the Nullable generic.

This page is intentionally left blank

Regular Expressions &
Exception Handling

114: Does C# support Regular Expressions?

Answer:

Yes.

115: Which of the following code sample best replaces ,http0//` with ,https0//`?

A. s = Regex.Replace(s, "http://", "https://");

B. s = Regex.Replace(s, "https://", "http://");

C. s = Regex.Replace(s, "http://", "https://", RegexOptions.IgnoreCase);

D. s = Regex.Replace(s, "https://", "http://", RegexOptions.IgnoreCase);

Answer:

Correct Answer is C.

This code sample correctly replaces ,http0//` with ,https0//` regardless of case.

116: How can I create my own Exception?

Answer:

You can create your own exception by deriving it from *System.Exception class.*

117: How can you find which line of code is throwing exception using exception *class*?

Answer:

The *StrackTrace* method of Exception *class* contains all code stacks with line number from where Exception has been thrown.

118: What is the correct order for Catch clauses when handling different exception types?

A. Order from most general to most specific.

B. Order from most likely to least likely to occur.

C. Order from most specific to most general.

D. Order from least likely to most likely to occur.

Answer:

Correct answer is C: The first type that matches is caught, and subsequent Catch clauses are skipped. Therefore, you should order Catch clauses from most specific to most general to enable you to catch errors that you have specific error-handling for, while still catching other exceptions with the more general Catch clauses.

119: What happens when you divide any number by zero?

Answer:

It will throw *System.DivideByZeroException* exception.

This page is intentionally left blank

Collections

120: Is it possible to store multiple data types in Array?

Answer:

No. All members of array must be of same type.

121: Explain difference between *System.Array.CopyTo()* and *System.Array.Clone()*?

Answer:

System.Array.CopyTo() performs a deep copy of an array.

System.Array.Clone() performs a shallow copy of an array.

122: In C#, we have multiple Catch Blocks. Can we also have multiple finally blocks?

Answer:

No. In C# you can only have single *finally* Block for each *Try* Clause. You can have multiple *catch* blocks to catch different exceptions.

123: When we declare Try Block, is it necessary to also Declare Finally Block?

Answer:

No. *Finally* Block is optional. If you don't want then you can omit it.

124: Which code segment will generate type safe dictionary class?

A *class* CustomDictionary : Dictionary<string, string>

B. *class* CustomDictionary : HashTable

C. *class* CustomDictionary : IDictionary

D. *class* CustomDictionary

{

Dictionary<string, string> dic = new Dictionary<string, string>();

}

Answer:

Correct Answer is A.

125: Which *class* is optimized for key based item retrieval from small and large collection objects?

A. OrderedDictionary *Class*

B. HybridDictionary *Class*

C. ListDictionary *Class*

D. HashTable *Class*

Answer:

Correct Answer is B.

126: What is *ArrayList*?

Answer:

An *Arraylist* is a simple resizeable, index-based collection of objects.

127: What is *HashTable Class*?

Answer:

Hashtable is a collection of name/value pairs of objects that allow retrieval by name or index.

128: What is *HybridDictionary*?

Answer:

A collection that uses a *ListDictionary* for storage when the number of items in the collection is small and then migrates the items to a *Hashtable* for large collections is called *HybridDictionary*.

129: What is a *Queue class*?

Answer:

A Queue represents a first-in, first-out collection of objects. Queues are useful for storing messages in the order they were received for sequential processing. This class implements a queue as a circular array. Objects stored in a Queue are inserted at one end and removed from the other.

130: What is a *Stack class*?

Answer:

A *Stack* represents a simple last-in-first-out (LIFO) non-generic collection of objects. Stack is implemented as a circular buffer. The capacity of a Stack is the number of elements the Stack can hold. As elements are added to a Stack, the capacity is automatically increased as required through reallocation.

131: Which of the following *ArrayList* methods can be used

to determine whether an item exists in the collection?

(Choose all that apply.)

A. *Remove*

B. *Contains*

C. *IndexOf*

D. *Count*

Answer:

Correct answers: B and C

B. *Contains* can be used to test whether the item exists in the collection.

C. *IndexOf* will return -1 if the item does not exist in the collection.

132: What does the Dequeue method of the Queue *class* do? (Choose all that apply.)

A. Retrieves an item from the front of the collection

B. Adds an item to the collection

C. Removes the first item from the collection

D. Clears the collection

Answer:

Correct answers: A and C

A. It does retrieve the item from the front of the collection.

C. As it retrieves an item, it also removes it from the collection.

133: In what order does a Stack retrieve items as you use its Pop method?

A. Random order

B. First-in, first-out

C. Last-in, first-out

D. Last-in, last-out

Answer:

Correct answer: C

Last-in, first-out

134: What kind of object does the generic Dictionary enumerator return?

A. Object

B. Generic KeyValuePair objects

C. Key

D. Value

Answer:

Correct answer: B

The enumerator is type-safe to return a *KeyValuePair*.

135: Where can you add items to a LinkedList? (Choose all that apply.)

A. At the beginning of the LinkedList

B. Before any specific node

C. After any specific node

D. At the end of the LinkedList

E. At any numeric index in the LinkedList

Answer:

Correct answers: A, B, C, and D

A. You can add at the beginning of the LinkedList.

B. You can add before a specific node in the LinkedList.

C. You can add after a specific node in the LinkedList.

D. You can add at the end of the LinkedList.

136: Does *ArrayList* support different types of objects in its collection?

Answer:

Yes. We can store different types of objects in *ArrayList*.

Any reference or value type that is added to an *ArrayList* is implicitly upcast to Object.

```
class Program
{
    static void Main(string[] args)
    {
        ArrayList list = new ArrayList();
        list.Add("ssss");
        list.Add(100);
        list.Add(false);
    }
}
```

137: Which interface is implemented by stack *class*?

Answer:

Stack *class* implements *ICollection* interface.

138: Which interface is implemented by List *class*?

Answer:

List *class* implements *IList* Interface.

139: What happens if you add item with the same key in dictionary?

Answer:

It will throw an error.

140: What happens if you add item with the same key in *hashtable*?

Answer:

It will simply replace item in its collection.

Garbage Collector

141: When will the garbage collector run?

A. Every 15 minutes.

B. Once every day at 13:00.

C. When the application is low on memory.

D. Randomly based on the resource load on the system.

Answer:

Correct answer is C. The garbage collector will only run when the application is running short on memory.

142: You are creating a generic *class*, and you need to dispose-off the generic objects. How can you do this?

A. Call the Object.Dispose method.

B. Implement the IDisposable interface.

C. Derive the generic *class* from the IDisposable *class*.

D. Use constraints to require the generic type to implement the Disposable interface.

Answer:

Correct answer is D.

If you use constraints to require types to implement a specific interface, you can call any method used in the interface.

143: What is the advantage of *using* statement?

Answer:

The *using* statement ensures that Dispose is called even if an exception occurs while you are calling methods on the object. You can achieve the same results by putting the object inside a try block and then calling Dispose in a finally block; in fact, this is how the *using* statement is translated by the compiler.

144: How can you call garbage collector through code?

Answer:

You can use *GC.Collect()* method. It forces garbage collection to occur immediately.

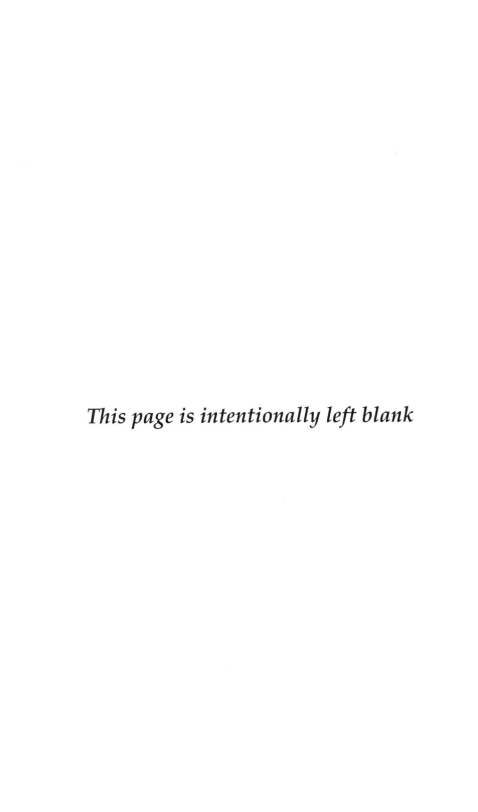

This page is intentionally left blank

File Handling

145: Which namespace contains all methods and classes related to Directory and File Handling?

Answer:

The *System.IO* namespace contains all classes and methods related to Directory and File Handling.

146: Which *class* contains methods related to Directory Operations like creating, moving & iterating?

Answer:

The *DirectoryInfo Class* from System.IO namespace contains all methods related to Directory operations.

147: What are the correct ways to open a file for writing?

A. *File.Open("somefile.txt", FileMode.Create);*

B. *File.Open("somefile.txt", FileMode.Create, FileAccess.Write);*

C. *File.Open("somefile.txt", FileMode.Create, FileAccess.Read);*

D. *FileInfo file = new FileInfo("somefile.txt");*

file.Open(FileMode.Create);

Answer:

Correct answers: A, B, and D

A. Not specifying the *FileAccess* on *File.Open* defaults to read/write access.

B. Explicitly using the *FileAccess.Write* value allows you to write to the file.

D. Creating a new *FileInfo* object and opening it with *FileMode.Create* defaults to read/write access to the file.

148: Determine the output of the following code segment:

int i = 20;

i++;

i += --i;

System.Console.WriteLine ("The value of i is : {0}", i);

A. 40

B. 41

C. 42

D. 39

Answer:

Correct answer is B.

i = 20 + 1 + (21 − 1) = 41

149. Which methods of the FileStream *class* affect the Position property? (Choose all that apply.)

A. Read

B. Lock

C. Write

D. Seek

Answer:

Correct answers: A, C, and D

A. This method reads from the file and moves the position forward.

C. This method writes to the file and moves the position forward.

D. This method moves the position to another place in the file.

150. Which of the following classes interact with the file system? (Choose all that apply.)

A. FileStream

B. MemoryStream

C. StringReader

D. StreamReader

E. SslStream

Answer:

Correct answers are A and D.

Delegates and Events

151: What is the use of Events?

Answer:

Events provide mechanism for a *class* or object to notify other classes or objects when something of interest occurs.

The *class* that sends (or raises) the event is called the *publisher* and the classes that receive (or handle) the event are called *subscribers*.

152: What is an EventHandler?

Answer:

EventHandler is a predefined delegate that specifically represents an event handler method for an event that does not generate data. If your event does generate data, you must supply your own custom event data type and either create a delegate where the type of the second parameter is your custom type, or use the generic *EventHandler<TEventArgs>* delegate *class* and substitute your custom type for the generic type parameter.

153: What is a Delegate?

Answer:

A *Delegate* is a reference type, like the other reference types; but instead of referring to an object, a *Delegate* refers to a method. This is known as *encapsulating the method*. When you create the delegate, you specify a method signature and return type; you can encapsulate any matching method with that delegate. The concept is somewhat similar to function pointers in C++.

154: Does delegate have any return type?

Answer:

Yes. *Delegate* has a return type.

155: Does event have any return type?

Answer:

No. *Event* cannot return anything.

156: What is Multicast Delegate?

Answer:

All Delegate instances have multicast capability. This means that a delegate instance can reference not just a single target method, but also a list of target methods. The += operator combines delegate instances.

delegateTest d = TestMethod1;
d += TestMethod2;

Invoking d will now call both *TestMethod1* and *TestMethod2*. Delegates are invoked in the order they are added.

157: Given the following code, what will the compiler do?

```
class MyPersonalTest
 {
   sealed abstract void TestMethod()
    {
      System.Console.WriteLine ("This is TestMethod ");
```

```
   }
 }
```

A. The code will compile properly.

B. The *class* visibility is incorrect.

C. System.Console.WriteLine is specified incorrectly.

D. TestMethod() is not properly declared.

Answer:

The correct answer is D. You cannot specify sealed and abstract in the same declaration.

158: What kind of delegate will be created for the following method?

public void TestMethod(object sender, System.EventArgs e)
```
 {
   <
 }
```
A. Single delegate

B. Event delegate

C. Multicast delegate

D. Proxy delegate

Answer:

The correct answer is C. Any delegate that is declared as public void is a multicast delegate.

159: The following code segment creates an event handler. What text must be inserted in place of << *blank* >> for the event to work?

```
//declare the delegate for the event
public delegate void PrintDocumentEventHandler();
public class Printer
 {
   // declare the Print event
   public <<blank>> event PrintDocumentEventHandler Print;
   // <
 }
```

A. void

B. delegate

C. combine

D. *static*

Answer:

The correct answer is D. Events must be declared as *static*.

160: You need to define a delegate for the following method:

public class Calculator

```
 {
   public static int MultiplyBy10(int counter)
   {
     return counter *10;
   }
 }
```

How is the delegate for *MultiplyBy10 ( )* declared?

A. delegate Calculator.MultiplyBy10;

B. delegate int MulBy10(int i);

C. delegate void MultiplyBy10(string s);

D. delegate int Calculator.MultiplyBy10(int i);

Answer:

Correct answer is B. The delegate should have the same signature as the method it will encapsulate, except that the name must be unique in the scope.

161: What is the purpose of a delegate?

A. To spawn an additional thread to provide parallel processing

B. To copy member methods and properties from an existing *class*

C. To enable an assembly to respond to an event that occurs within a *class*

D. To provide identical member methods and properties from multiple related classes

Answer:

Correct answer is C.

Globalization/Localization

162: What is the name given to the type of assembly that contains localized resources?

A. Spoke

B. Hub

C. Sputnik

D. Satellite

Answer:

Correct answer is D.

163: What namespace contains the ResourceManager *class?*

A. System.Localization

B. System.Resources

C. System.Globalization

D. System.Threading

Answer:

Correct answer is B.

164: Explain the term Fallback resource/fallback locale.

Answer:

The *fallback locale (resource)* is the locale that will be used when there are no resources for the user's locale.

165: What happens when the Resource Manager fails to find the localized resource for a locale?

A. It uses the closest locale.

B. It throws an exception.

C. Nothing, the resource will be blank.

D. It uses the fallback resource.

Answer:

Correct answer is D.

166: Explain the term Localization.

Answer:

The process of enabling an application to format numbers and dates based on a specific locale is called *localization*.

167: Which namespace contains the CultureInfo *class*?

A. System.Localization

B. System.Resources

C. System.Globalization

D. System.Threading

Answer:

Correct answer is C.

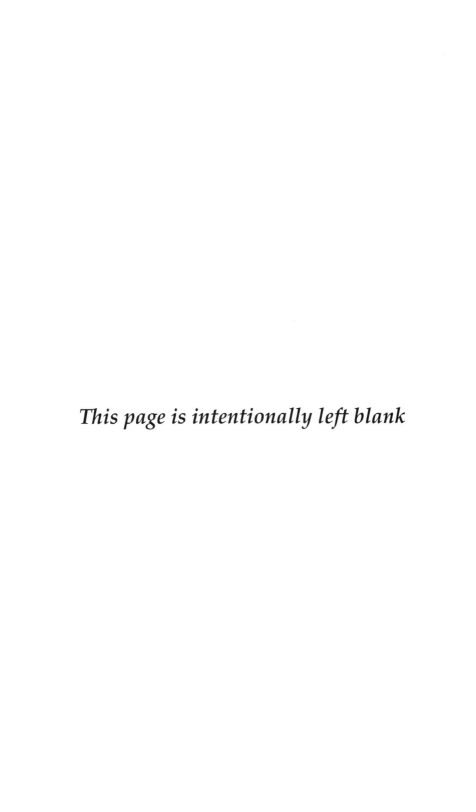

This page is intentionally left blank

Threading, Interfaces & Serialization

168: How can you get list of all processes running on current system?

Answer:

The Process *class* has a method named *GetProcesses* that helps you get a list of all processes running on your system. e.g *Process.GetProcesses()*

169: Is it possible to kill any process from application?

Answer:

Yes, you can use *Kill()* method to kill any process from your application.

170: Explain use of lock statement in C#.

Answer:

Lock statement is a statement that allows only one thread (at a time) to execute a block of code. It is generally used when one is designing a multi threaded application.

171: How can we set thread to run in background?

Answer:

You can use *IsBackground* property of thread to achieve this.

172: What does Sleep method do in context of thread?

Answer:

Sleep method blocks the current thread for a certain amount of time. It relinquishes execution to other threads to allow them to do work.

173: Which method stops a running thread?

A. Thread.Suspend

B. Thread.Resume

C. Thread.Abort

D. Thread.Join

Answer:

Correct answer: C

C. The *Thread.Abort* method tells the thread to stop by firing a *ThreadAbortException*.

174: Which of the following are valid reasons to create an application domain? (Choose all that apply.)

A. It is the only way to launch a separate process.

B. You can remove the application domain to free up resources.

C. Application domains improve performance.

D. Application domains provide a layer of separation and security.

Answer:

Correct answers: B and D

B. You can call *AppDomain.Unload* to close the application domain and free up resources.

D. Application domains provide a layer of separation. Additionally/ you can limit the application domain's privileges/

reducing the risk of a security vulnerability being exploited in an assembly.

175: What is the use of IComparable interface?

Answer:

IComparable interface is required for sorting. It should be implemented by types whose values can be ordered.

176: What is use of IDisposable interface?

Answer:

The primary use of this interface is to release unmanaged resources.

Use the *Dispose* method of this interface to explicitly release unmanaged resources in conjunction with the garbage collector. The consumer of an object can call this method when the object is no longer needed.

177: What is the difference between IDictionary and IList Interface?

Answer:

IDictionary and *IList* both extend *ICollection* Interface.

An *IDictionary* implementation is a collection of key/value pairs, like the *Hashtable class*.

An *IList* implementation is a collection of values and its members can be accessed by index, like the *ArrayList class*.

178: Why do we have to use IEnumerable Interface?

Answer:

IEnumerable Interface exposes the enumerator, which supports a simple iteration over a non-generic collection. So we can easily iterate over object collection.

179: Which of the following attributes should you add to a *class* to enable it to be serialized?

A. ISerializable

B. Serializable

C. SoapInclude

D. OnDeserialization

Answer:

Correct answer: B

B. Classes must have the *Serializable* attribute to be serialized.

180: Which of the following are requirements for a *class* to be serialized with XML serialization? (Choose all that apply.)

A. The *class* must be public.

B. The *class* must be private.

C. The *class* must have a parameterless constructor.

D. The *class* must have a constructor that accepts a SerializationInfo parameter.

Answer:

Correct answers: A and C

A. Classes serialized with XML serialization must be public.

C. For XML serialization to work, the *class* must have a parameterless constructor.

181: Which kind of classes do not serialize?

Answer:

Any *class* implementing *ICollection* interface cannot be serialized.

New Features

182: Explain the term Anonymous types.

Answer:

Anonymous types provide a convenient way to encapsulate a set of read-only properties into a single object without having to first explicitly define a type. The type name is generated by the compiler and is not available at the source code level.
The following example shows an anonymous type being initialized with two properties called FirstName and LastName.

var v = new { FirstName = ,Stever`/ LastName= "Joe" };

183: Can we declare methods or events in Anonymous types?

Answer:

No. Anonymous types consist of only one or more public read-only properties. No other kinds of *class* members such as methods or events are allowed. An anonymous type cannot be cast to any interface or type except for object.

184: Is it possible to give a name to Anonymous type?

Answer:

No. It is not possible to give a name to *Anonymous type*. It is only generated by compiler.

185: What is the scope of Anonymous type?

Answer:

An *Anonymous type* has only method scope. If you want to pass outside the method then you will have to convert it to an object.

186: What are Extension Methods?

Answer:

Extension Methods enable you to "add" methods to existing types without creating a new derived type, recompiling, or otherwise modifying the original type. Extension methods are a special kind of *static* method, but they are called as if they were instance methods on the extended type.

For client code, there is no apparent difference between calling an extension method and the methods that are actually defined in a type.

187: Can we declare Extension method with the same name as a method defined in the type?

Answer:

Yes, it is possible. But an extension method will never be called if it has the same signature as a method defined in the type.

188: Give example of any Extension method.

Answer:

Below is an example which will define extension method *removeHTML* on string type:

```
public static class Extension
{
  public static void removeHTML(this string str)
  {
    Console.WriteLine("removeHTML Extension method on string");
  }
}
```

You can call extension method as following:

```
class Program
{
  static void Main(string[] args)
  {
    string str = " ";
    str.removeHTML();
  }
}
```

189: What is the use of Partial Keyword?

Answer:

The *Partial Keyword* indicates that other parts of the *class, struct,* or interface can be defined in the namespace.

It is possible to split the definition of a *class* or a *struct,* an interface or a method over two or more source files. Each source file contains a section of the type or method definition, and all parts are combined when the application is compiled. All the parts must use the partial keyword.

All the parts must be available at compile time to form the final type. All the parts must have the same accessibility, such as public, private, and so on.

190: What happens if any part of partial *class* is declared as abstract?

Answer:

If any part is declared abstract, then the whole type is considered abstract.

191: What happens if any part of partial *class* is declared as sealed?

Answer:

If any part is declared sealed, then the whole type is considered as sealed.

192: If we want to inherit partial *class* from any base *class*, do we have to inherit it in all declaration?

Answer:

No. You can inherit base *class* in any part of partial declaration. There is no need to inherit it in all parts.

193: What is the use of Activator *Class*?

Answer:

The *Activator class* contains methods to create types of objects locally or remotely, or obtain references to existing remote objects. This *class* cannot be inherited.

194: You have a name of Type, how can you generator instance of that type?

Answer:

The Activator *class* contains a *static* method called *CreateInstance()*, which will be used to generate an instance of type.

195: What is Metadata?

Answer:

In general, *Metadata* is information about the types defined in a program. It is data about data.

Metadata is binary information describing your program that is stored either in a Common Language Runtime Portable Executable (PE) file or in memory. When you compile your code into a PE file, metadata is inserted into one portion of the file, while your code is converted to Microsoft Intermediate Language (MSIL) and inserted into another portion of the file. Every type and member defined and referenced in a module or assembly is described within metadata. When code is executed, the runtime loads metadata into memory and references it to discover information about your code's classes, members, inheritance, and so on.

196: What is Attribute *Class*?

Answer:

Attributes provide a powerful method of associating metadata, or declarative information, with code (assemblies, types, methods, properties, and so forth). After an attribute is associated with a program entity, the attribute can be queried at run time by using a technique called *Reflection*.

197: Can you declare attribute on Property?

Answer:

Yes. You can declare attribute at assembly, type, method, property and so on levels.

198: Does attribute declaration allows parameters?

Answer:

Yes. You can pass parameters in attribute declaration.

199: I have developed new version of my *class* library. I want that my new users don't use old methods; instead they use new method/ still I don't want to break code of old users who use old method. How can I achieve this?

Answer:

You have to mark old method with *[System.Obsolete]* attribute, so user knows this method is obsolete and no more in use.

200: What is the use of Reflection?

Answer:

Reflection enables you to obtain information about loaded assemblies and the types defined within them, such as classes, interfaces, and value types. You can also use *reflection* to create type instances at run time, and to invoke and access them.

This page is intentionally left blank

HR Questions

Review these typical interview questions and think about how you would answer them. Read the answers listed; you will find best possible answers along with strategies and suggestions.

This page is intentionally left blank

1: Tell me about yourself?

Answer:

The most often asked question in interviews. You need to have a short statement prepared in your mind. Keep your answer to one or two minutes. Don't ramble. Be careful that it does not sound rehearsed. Limit it to work-related items unless instructed otherwise. Talk about things you have done and jobs you have held that relate to the position you are interviewing for. Start with the item farthest back and work up to the present (If you have a profile or personal statement(s) at the top of your CV use this as your starting point).

2: Why did you leave your last job?

Answer:

Stay positive regardless of the circumstances. Never refer to a major problem with management and never speak ill of supervisors, co- workers or the organization. If you do, you will be the one looking bad. Keep smiling and talk about leaving for a positive reason such as an opportunity, a chance to do something special or other forward- looking reasons.

3: What experience do you have in this field?

Answer:

Speak about specifics that relate to the position you are applying for. If you do not have specific experience, get as close as you can.

4: Do you consider yourself successful?

Answer:

You should always answer yes and briefly explain why. A good explanation is that you have set goals, and you have met some and are on track to achieve the others.

5: What do co-workers say about you?

Answer:

Be prepared with a quote or two from co-workers. Either a specific statement or a paraphrase will work. Bill Smith, a co-worker at Clarke Company, always said I was the hardest worker's he had ever known. It should be as powerful as Bill having said it at the interview herself.

6: What do you know about this organization?

Answer:

This question is one reason to do some research on the organization before the interview. Research the company's products, size, reputation, Image, goals, problems, management style, skills, History and philosophy. Be informed and interested. Find out where they have been and where they are going. What are the current issues and who are the major players?

7: What have you done to improve your knowledge in the last year?

Answer:

Try to include improvement activities that relate to the job. A wide variety of activities can be mentioned as positive self-improvement. Have some good ones handy to mention.

8: Are you applying for other jobs?

Answer:

Be honest but do not spend a lot of time in this area. Keep the focus on this job and what you can do for this organization. Anything else is a distraction.

9: Why do you want to work for this organization?

Answer:

This may take some thought and certainly, should be based on the research you have done on the organization. Sincerity is extremely important here and will easily be sensed. Relate it to your long-term career goals. Never talk about what you want; first talk about their Needs. You want to be part of an exciting forward-moving company. You can make a definite contribution to specific company goals.

10: Do you know anyone who works for us?

Answer:

Be aware of the policy on relatives working for the organization. This can affect your answer even though they asked about friends not relatives. Be careful to mention a friend only if they are well thought of.

11: What kind of salary do you need?

Answer:

A loaded question! A nasty little game that you will probably lose if you answer first. So, do not answer it. Instead, say something like/ that's a tough question. Can you tell me the range for this position? In most cases, the interviewer, taken off guard, will tell you. If not, say that it can depend on the details of the job. Then give a wide range.

12: Are you a team player?

Answer:

You are, of course, a team player. Be sure to have examples ready. Specifics that show you often perform for the good of the team rather than for yourself is good evidence of your team attitude. Do not brag; just say it in a matter-of-fact tone. This is a key point.

13: How long would you expect to work for us if hired?

Answer:

Specifics here are not good. Something like this should work: I'd like it to be a long time. Or As long as we both feel I'm doing a good job.

14: Have you ever had to fire anyone? How did you feel about

that?

Answer:

This is serious. Do not make light of it or in any way seem like you like to fire people. At the same time, you will do it when it is the right thing to do. When it comes to the organization versus the individual who has created a harmful situation, you will protect the organization. Remember firing is not the same as layoff or reduction in force.

15: What is your philosophy towards work?

Answer:

The interviewer is not looking for a long or flowery dissertation here. Do you have strong feelings that the job gets done? Yes. That's the type of answer that works best here. Keep it short and positive, showing a benefit to the organization.

16: If you had enough money to retire right now, would you?

Answer:

Answer yes if you would. But since you need to work, this is the type of work you prefer. Do not say yes if you do not mean it.

17: Have you ever been asked to leave a position?

Answer:

If you have not, say no. If you have, be honest, brief and avoid saying negative things about the people or organization involved.

18: Explain how you would be an asset to this organization.

Answer:

You should be anxious for this question. It gives you a chance to highlight your best points as they relate to the position being discussed. Give a little advance thought to this relationship.

19: Why should we hire you?

Answer:

Point out how your assets meet what the organization needs. Also mention about your knowledge, experience, abilities, and skills. Never mention any other candidates to make a comparison.

20: Tell me about a suggestion you have made.

Answer:

Have a good one ready. Be sure and use a suggestion that was accepted and was then considered successful. One related to the type of work applied for is a real plus.

21: What irritates you about co-workers?

Answer:

This is a trap question. Think real hard but fail to come up with anything that irritates you. A short statement that you seem to get along with folks is great.

22: What is your greatest strength?

Answer:

Numerous answers are good, just stay positive. A few good examples: Your ability to prioritize, Your problem-solving skills, Your ability to work under pressure, Your ability to focus on projects, Your professional expertise, Your leadership skills, Your positive attitude

23: Tell me about your dream job or what are you looking for in a job?

Answer:

Stay away from a specific job. You cannot win. If you say the job you are contending for is it, you strain credibility. If you say another job is it, you plant the suspicion that you will be dissatisfied with this position if hired. The best is to stay genetic and say something like: A job where I love the work, like the people, can contribute and can't wait to get to work.

24: Why do you think you would do well at this job?

Answer:

Give several reasons and include skills, experience and interest.

25: What do you find the most attractive about this position (Least attractive)?

Answer:

a) List a couple of attractive factors such as the responsibility the post offers and the opportunity to work with experienced teams that have a reputation for innovation and creativity.

b) Say you'd need more information and time before being able to make a judgment on any unattractive aspects.

26: What kind of person would you refuse to work with?
Answer:
Do not be trivial. It would take disloyalty to the organization, violence or lawbreaking to get you to object. Minor objections will label you as a whiner.

27: What is more important to you: the money or the work?
Answer:
Money is always important, but the work is the most important. There is no better answer.

28: What would your previous supervisor say your strongest point is?
Answer:
There are numerous good possibilities:
Loyalty, Energy, Positive attitude, Leadership, Team player, Expertise, Initiative, Patience, Hard work, Creativity, Problem solver.

29: Tell me about a problem you had with a supervisor.

Answer:

Biggest trap of all! This is a test to see if you will speak ill of your boss. If you fall for it and tell about a problem with a former boss, you may well below the interview right there. Stay positive and develop a poor memory about any trouble with a supervisor.

30: What has disappointed you about a job?

Answer:

Don't get trivial or negative. Safe areas are few but can include: Not enough of a challenge. You were laid off in a reduction Company did not win a contract, which would have given you more responsibility.

31: Tell me about your ability to work under pressure.

Answer:

You may say that you thrive under certain types of pressure. Give an example that relates to the type of position applied for.

32: Do your skills match this job or another job more closely?

Answer:

Probably this one! Do not give fuel to the suspicion that you may want another job more than this one.

33: What motivates you to do your best on the job?

Answer:

This is a personal trait that only you can say, but good examples are: Challenge, Achievement, and Recognition.

34: Are you willing to work overtime? Nights? Weekends?

Answer:

This is up to you. Be totally honest.

35: How would you know you were successful on this job?

Answer:

Several ways are good measures:

You set high standards for yourself and meet them. Your outcomes are a success. Your boss tells you that you are successful and doing a great job.

36: Would you be willing to relocate if required?

Answer:

You should be clear on this with your family prior to the interview if you think there is a chance it may come up. Do not say yes just to get the job if the real answer is no. This can create a lot of problems later on in your career. Be honest at this point. This will save you from future grief.

37: Are you willing to put the interests of the organization ahead of your own?

Answer:

This is a straight loyalty and dedication question. Do not worry about the deep ethical and philosophical implications. Just say yes.

38: Describe your management style.

Answer:

Try to avoid labels. Some of the more common labels, like progressive, salesman or consensus, can have several meanings or descriptions depending on which management expert you listen to. The situational style is safe, because it says you will manage according to the situation, instead of one size fits all.

39: What have you learned from mistakes on the job?

Answer:

Here you have to come up with something or you strain credibility. Make it small, well intentioned mistake with a positive lesson learned. An example would be, working too far ahead of colleagues on a project and thus throwing coordination off.

40: Do you have any blind spots?

Answer:

Trick question! If you know about blind spots, they are no longer blind spots. Do not reveal any personal areas of concern here. Let them do their own discovery on your bad points. Do not hand it to them.

41: If you were hiring a person for this job, what would you look for?

Answer:

Be careful to mention traits that are needed and that you have.

42: Do you think you are overqualified for this position?

Answer:

Regardless of your qualifications, state that you are very well qualified for the position you've been interviewed for.

43: How do you propose to compensate for your lack of experience?

Answer:

First, if you have experience that the interviewer does not know about, bring that up: Then, point out (if true) that you are a hard working quick learner.

44: What qualities do you look for in a boss?

Answer:

Be generic and positive. Safe qualities are knowledgeable, a sense of humor, fair, loyal to subordinates and holder of high standards. All bosses think they have these traits.

45: Tell me about a time when you helped resolve a dispute between others.

Answer:

Pick a specific incident. Concentrate on your problem solving technique and not the dispute you settled.

46: What position do you prefer on a team working on a project?

Answer:

Be honest. If you are comfortable in different roles, point that out.

47: Describe your work ethic.

Answer:

Emphasize benefits to the organization. Things like, determination to get the job done and work hard but enjoy your work are good.

48: What has been your biggest professional disappointment?

Answer:

Be sure that you refer to something that was beyond your control. Show acceptance and no negative feelings.

49: Tell me about the most fun you have had on the job.

Answer:

Talk about having fun by accomplishing something for the organization.

50: What would you do for us? (What can you do for us that someone else can't?)

a) Relate past experiences that represent success in Working for your previous employer.

b) Talk about your fresh perspective and the relevant experience you can bring to the company.

c) Highlight your track record of providing creative, Workable solutions.

51: Do you have any questions for me?

Answer:

Always have some questions prepared. Questions prepared where you will be an asset to the organization are good. How soon will I be able to be productive? What type of projects will I be able to assist on?

And Finally Good Luck!

INDEX

C# Questions

OOPS - Theory

1: Does C# support *Static* Constructor?

2: How can you implement multiple inheritances in C#?

3: C# provides default constructor, I will write my own const-ructor with string argument. I don't want to allow anyone from outside to call default constructor. Can I achieve it?

4: Is it possible to override private virtual methods?

5: How can you make sure that your *class* can not be inherited by any other *class*?

6: Can you declare a private member in an Interface *Class*?

7: Are *static* indexers allowed in C#?

8: Can I provide different access modifiers on get/set methods of a property?

9: Which of the following statements is true?

10: Is it possible to create an instance of an Abstract *Class*?

11: Can I have a Concrete method in Abstract *Class*?

12: Can I declare *Static* Variable inside Method Block?

13: Which of the following statements are true? (Choose all that apply.)

14: What do you mean by Interface Mapping?

15: What is the difference between *structs* and *classes*?

16: Explain scope of Private Access Modifier.

17: Explain scope of Protected Access Modifier.

18: Explain scope of Internal Access Modifier.

19: Can we inherit *struct*?

20: Is it possible to declare member as Protected in *Struct*?

21: Can we declare *const* or *static* members in Interface?

22: Can we create an object of an Interface?

23: What is the difference between *Readonly* and *Const* field?

24: What is nested type?

25: What is default accessibility of nested type?

26: What are Destructors?

27: Can we define destructor in *Struct*?

28: Can we have multiple destructors in a *class*?

29: Can we pass parameters in a destructor?

30: Can we call a destructor by coding?

31: Is overloading possible when methods have different return types but have same signature?

32: What is Method Overloading?

OOPS - Syntax

33: Please select correct syntax for implementing Interface in C#.

34: Given the following code, what will the compiler do?

Language - Theory

35: What is the use of *volatile* keyword?

36: What is the use of *extern modifier*?

37: What is the difference between extern and abstract modifier?

38: What is Indexer?

39: Is the *'#include'* statement in C++ same as *'using'* statement in C#?

40: What is the output format of the file produced by the C# compiler?

41: Is there any difference between C++ reference and C# reference?

42: How can I get the name of a type at run time?

43: How can I do case insensitive string comparison?

44: What is the difference between == and *object.Equals*?

45: What is the implicit name of the parameter that gets passed to the *class'* set method?

46: How many styles of commenting are supported by C#?

47: Explain the terms: Shallow copy, Deep Copy.

48: Explain the term: Immutable.

49: How can I declare Constant variable in C#?

50: Can I change *const* variable in my code?

51: I want to initialize a constant variable, whose value is calculated on other two variables, out of which one is constant and other is a normal variable. What will happen?

52: Given the following program, what is the outcome when you try to compile and run it?

53: What is the correct declaration of *static* method?

54: With which of the following statement(s) you can replace *multiple if* statement in C#?

55: Which of the following is not a C# keyword?

56: Given the following code segment, what is the content of the string *s* in line 4?

57: Explain the term: Implicit Conversions.

58: Can I declare a variable called ,12Question` of type str ing in C#?

59: Can I Declare 2 variables called ,variabel1` and ,Variable1` in single method?

60: Is it necessary to write default block in Switch Statement?

61: What will be the return type of String.Compare() method?

62: Does C# support optional parameters?

63: Is it required to overload *!=* operator when we overload *==* operator?

64: What is the use of checked & unchecked statements in C#?

65: In C#, can we have two classes with same name in one application?

66: What Is Type forwarding?

67: What is the use of sizeof operator?

68: Can we get size in bytes for our custom *class* with sizeof operator?

69: Why sizeof keyword is considered as operator not a function?

70: Explain *params* keyword.

71: I want to declare a method which takes N number of arguments. How

72: Give any example where *params* keyword is used in method declaration.

73: What is the use of *ref* keyword?

74: Can we pass Value Types using *ref* keyword?

75: Is it necessary to initialize variable which will be passed by *ref* keyword?

76: What is the use of *out* keyword?

77: If both *out* and *ref* keywords pass argument by reference, what is the difference?

78: Will the following code compile?

79: Can we pass properties as a method argument using *ref* or *out* modifiers?

80: What is Strong Reference?

81: What is the use of *??* operator?

82: What is *Casting* or *Type Casting* or *Explicit Conversion*?

83: What is the use of Explicit Keyword?

84: What is the use of ,*i s*` keyword?

85: What is the use of ,*as*` keyword?

86: What is the use of *?:* Operator?

87: What is the use of *new* modifier in method?

88: What is the use of *yield* operator?

89: Explain the difference between *Parse, TryParse And Convert.*

90: Which namespace must be used in order to use the DOM for XML support?

91: Which namespace will be used to perform mathematical calculations?

Language - Syntax

92: Do these two statements generate same output?

93: What will be the output of following code segment?

Data Types

94: What is *ValueType*?

95: Can we inherit *ValueType* to create new derived type?

96: What is *ReferenceType*?

97: What is the default value of *int* type?

98: What is the default value of *bool* type?

99: What is the process of converting primitive type to *class* called?

100: Which Data type is suitable for finance and monetary calculations?

101: What is the default value of DateTime Variable?

102: How can you get current Date and Time?

103: What is the base *class* of all Enum types?

104: How is the Value Type stored in memory?

105: How is the Reference Type stored in memory?

106: Which of the following is not a Value Type? (Choose all that apply)

107: Which of the following is not a Reference Type? (Choose all that apply)

Nullable Types

108: What are Nullable Types?

109: Can we create a Nullable Type of Reference Type?

110: What are the possible values of Nullable Boolean Type?

111: How can you check whether Nullable variable has a value or is null?

112: What are the two possible ways of declaring Nullable Type in C#?

113: Which of the following is the correct declaration for a nullable integer?

Regular Expressions & Exception Handling

114: Does C# support Regular Expressions?

115: Which of the following code sample best replaces ,http0//` with

,https0//`?

116: How can I create my own Exception?

117: How can you find which line of code is throwing exception using exception *class*?

118: What is the correct order for Catch clauses when handling different exception types?

119: What happens when you divide any number by zero?

Collections

120: Is it possible to store multiple data types in Array?

121: Explain difference between *System.Array.CopyTo()* and *System.Array.Clone()*?

122: In C#, we have multiple Catch Blocks. Can we also have multiple finally blocks?

123: When we declare Try Block, is it necessary to also Declare Finally Block?

124: Which code segment will generate type safe dictionary *class*?

125: Which *class* is optimized for key based item retrieval from small and large collection objects?

126: What is *ArrayList*?

127: What is *HashTable Class*?

128: What is *HybridDictionary*?

129: What is a *Queue class*?

130: What is a *Stack class*?

131: Which of the following *ArrayList* methods can be used to determine whether an item exists in the collection? (Choose all that apply.)

132: What does the Dequeue method of the Queue *class* do? (Choose all that apply.)

133: In what order does a Stack retrieve items as you use its Pop method?

134: What kind of object does the generic Dictionary enumerator return?

135: Where can you add items to a LinkedList? (Choose all that apply.)

136: Does *ArrayList* support different types of objects in its collection?

137: Which interface is implemented by stack *class*?

138: Which interface is implemented by List *class*?

139: What happens if you add item with the same key in dictionary?

140: What happens if you add item with the same key in *hashtable*?

Garbage Collector

141: When will the garbage collector run?

142: You are creating a generic *class*, and you need to dispose-off the generic objects. How can you do this?

143: What is the advantage of *using* statement?

144: How can you call garbage collector through code?

File Handling

145: Which namespace contains all methods and classes related to Directory and File Handling?

146: Which *class* contains methods related to Directory Operations like creating, moving & iterating?

147: What are the correct ways to open a file for writing?

148: Determine the output of the following code segment:

149. Which methods of the FileStream *class* affect the Position property?

150. Which of the following classes interact with the file system? (Choose all that apply.)

Delegates and Events

151: What is the use of Events?

152: What is an EventHandler?

153: What is a Delegate?

154: Does delegate have any return type?

155: Does event have any return type?

156: What is Multicast Delegate?

157: Given the following code, what will the compiler do?

158: What kind of delegate will be created for the following method?

159: The following code segment creates an event handler. What text must be inserted in place of << *blank* >> for the event to work?

160: You need to define a delegate for the following method:

161: What is the purpose of a delegate?

Globalization/Localization

162: What is the name given to the type of assembly that contains localized resources?

163: What namespace contains the ResourceManager *class*?

164: Explain the term Fallback resource/fallback locale.

165: What happens when the Resource Manager fails to find the localized resource for a locale?

166: Explain the term Localization.

167: Which namespace contains the CultureInfo *class*?

Threading, Interfaces & Serialization

168: How can you get list of all processes running on current system?

169: Is it possible to kill any process from application?

170: Explain use of lock statement in C#.

171: How can we set thread to run in background?

172: What does Sleep method do in context of thread?

173: Which method stops a running thread?

174: Which of the following are valid reasons to create an application domain? (Choose all that apply.)

175: What is the use of IComparable interface?

176: What is use of IDisposable interface?

177: What is the difference between IDictionary and IList Interface?

178: Why do we have to use IEnumerable Interface?

179: Which of the following attributes should you add to a *class* to enable it to be serialized?

180: Which of the following are requirements for a *class* to be serialized with XML serialization? (Choose all that apply.)

181: Which kind of classes do not serialize?

New Features

182: Explain the term Anonymous types.

183: Can we declare methods or events in Anonymous types?

184: Is it possible to give a name to Anonymous type?

185: What is the scope of Anonymous type?

186: What are Extension Methods?

187: Can we declare Extension method with the same name as a method defined in the type?

188: Give example of any Extension method.

189: What is the use of Partial Keyword?

190: What happens if any part of partial *class* is declared as abstract?

191: What happens if any part of partial *class* is declared as sealed?

192: If we want to inherit partial *class* from any base *class*, do we have to inherit it in all declaration?

193: What is the use of Activator *Class*?

194: You have a name of Type, how can you generator instance of that type?

195: What is Metadata?

196: What is Attribute *Class*?

197: Can you declare attribute on Property?

198: Does attribute declaration allows parameters?

199: I have developed new version of my *class* library. I want that my new users don't use old methods; instead they use new method/ still I don't want to break code of old users who use old method. How can I achieve this?

200: What is the use of Reflection?

HR Questions

1: Tell me about yourself?

2: Why did you leave your last job?

3: What experience do you have in this field?

4: Do you consider yourself successful?

5: What do co-workers say about you?

6: What do you know about this organization?

7: What have you done to improve your knowledge in the last year?

8: Are you applying for other jobs?

9: Why do you want to work for this organization?

10: Do you know anyone who works for us?

11: What kind of salary do you need?

12: Are you a team player?

13: How long would you expect to work for us if hired?

14: Have you ever had to fire anyone? How did you feel about that?

15: What is your philosophy towards work?

16: If you had enough money to retire right now, would you?

17: Have you ever been asked to leave a position?

18: Explain how you would be an asset to this organization.

19: Why should we hire you?

20: Tell me about a suggestion you have made.

21: What irritates you about co-workers?

22: What is your greatest strength?

23: Tell me about your dream job or what are you looking for in a job?

24: Why do you think you would do well at this job?

25: What do you find the most attractive about this position? (Least attractive?)

26: What kind of person would you refuse to work with?

27: What is more important to you: the money or the work?

28: What would your previous supervisor say your strongest point is?

29: Tell me about a problem you had with a supervisor.

30: What has disappointed you about a job?

31: Tell me about your ability to work under pressure.

32: Do your skills match this job or another job more closely?

33: What motivates you to do your best on the job?

34: Are you willing to work overtime? Nights? Weekends?

35: How would you know you were successful on this job?

36: Would you be willing to relocate if required?

37: Are you willing to put the interests of the organization ahead of your own?

38: Describe your management style.

39: What have you learned from mistakes on the job?

40: Do you have any blind spots?

41: If you were hiring a person for this job, what would you look for?

42: Do you think you are overqualified for this position?

43: How do you propose to compensate for your lack of experience?

44: What qualities do you look for in a boss?

45: Tell me about a time when you helped resolve a dispute between others.

46: What position do you prefer on a team working on a project?

47: Describe your work ethic.

48: What has been your biggest professional disappointment?

49: Tell me about the most fun you have had on the job.

50: What would you do for us? (What can you do for us that someone else can't?)

51: Do you have any questions for me?

Some of the following titles might also be handy:

1. Oracle / PLSQL Interview Questions
2. ASP.NET Interview Questions
3. VB.NET Interview Questions
4. .NET Framework Interview Questions
5. C#.NET Interview Questions
6. OOPS Interview Questions
7. Core Java Interview Questions
8. JSP-Servlet Interview Questions
9. EJB (J2EE) Interview Questions
10. ADO.NET Interview Questions
11. SQL Server Interview Questions
12. C & C++ Interview Questions
13. 200 (HR) Interview Questions
14. JavaScript Interview Questions
15. JAVA/J2EE Interview Questions
16. Oracle DBA Interview Questions
17. XML Interview Questions
18. UNIX Shell Programming Interview Questions
19. PHP Interview Questions
20. J2ME Interview Questions
21. Hardware and Networking Interview Questions
22. Data Structures & Algorithms Interview Questions
23. Oracle E-Business Suite Interview Questions
24. UML Interview Questions
25. HTML, XHTML & CSS Interview Questions
26. JDBC Interview Questions
27. Hibernate, Springs & Struts Interview Questions
28. Linux Interview Questions

For complete list visit

www.vibrantpublishers.com

NOTES